SCHUBERT
QUINTET IN A MAJOR
"THE TROUT"

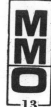

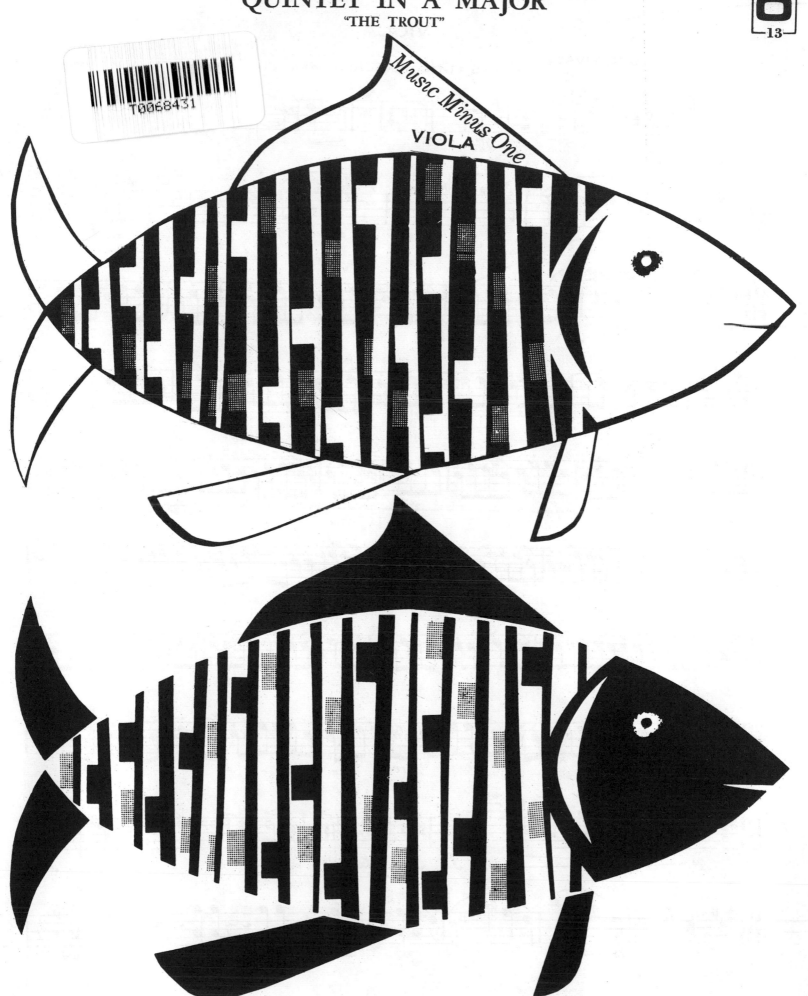

VIOLA

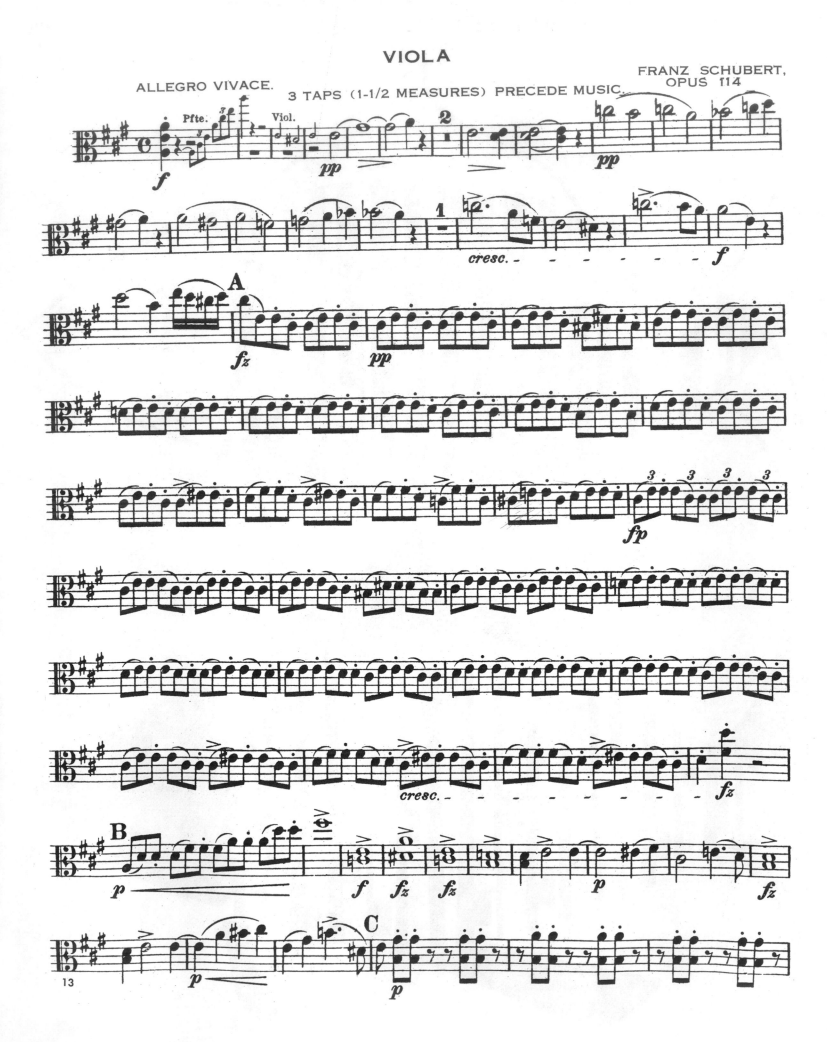

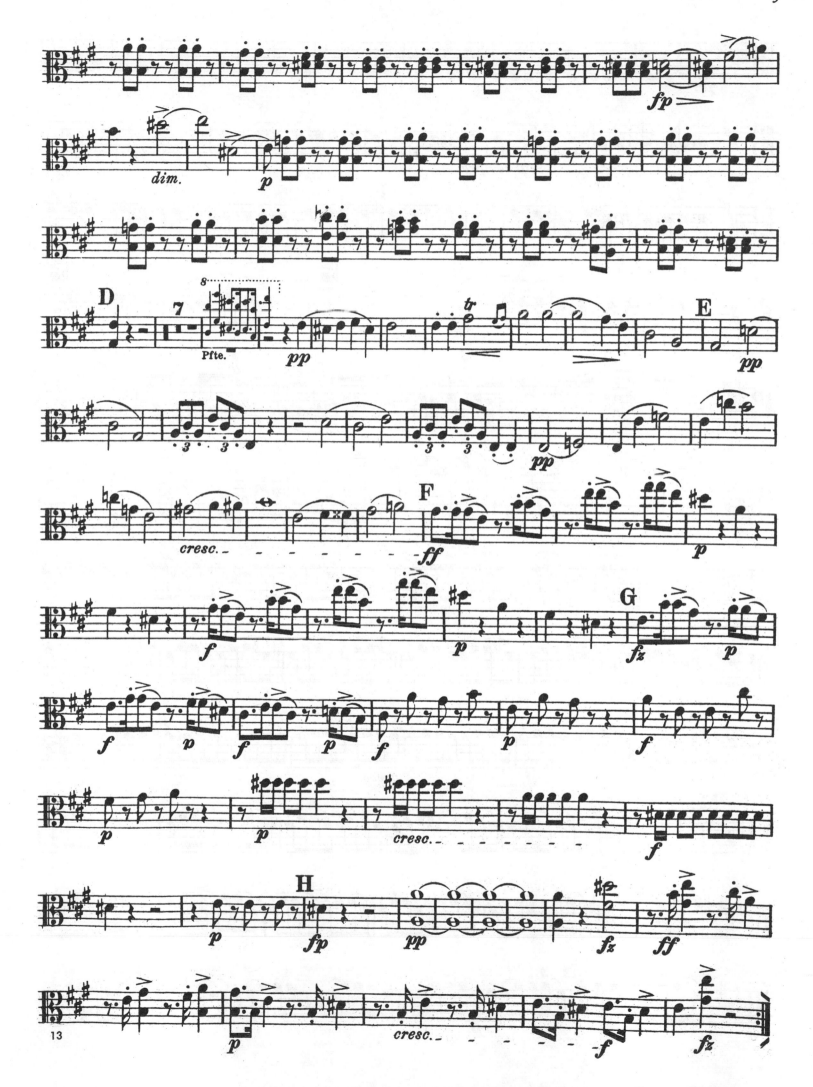

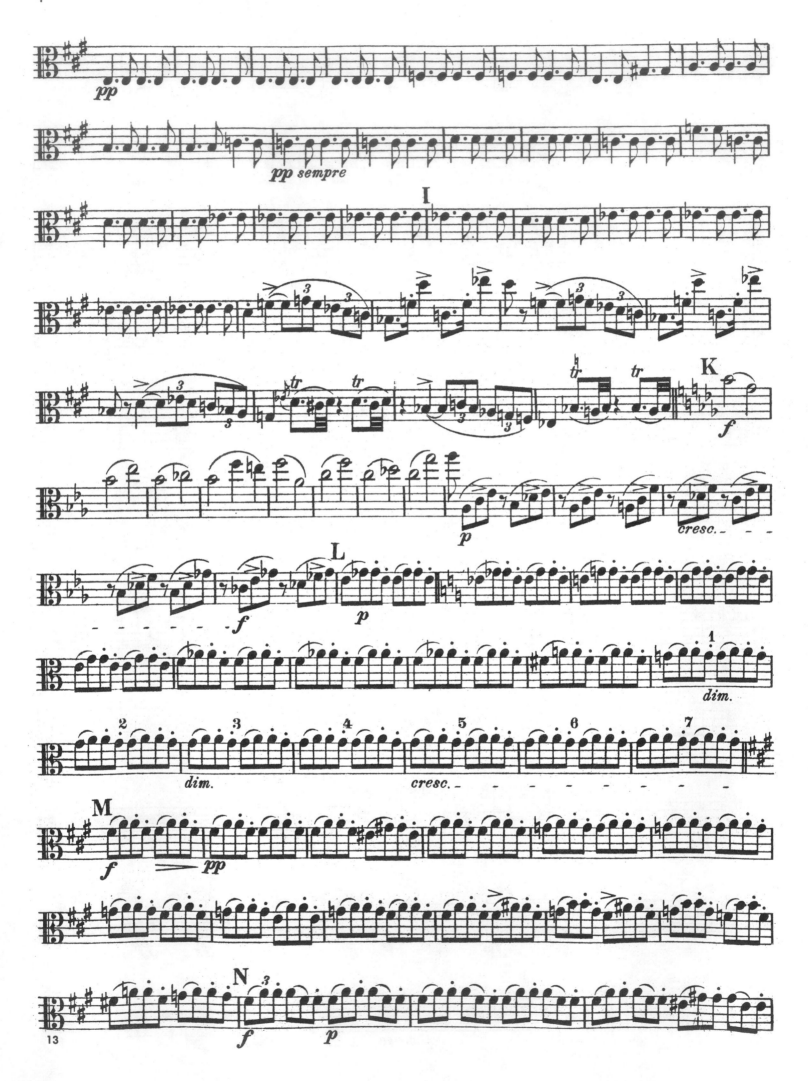

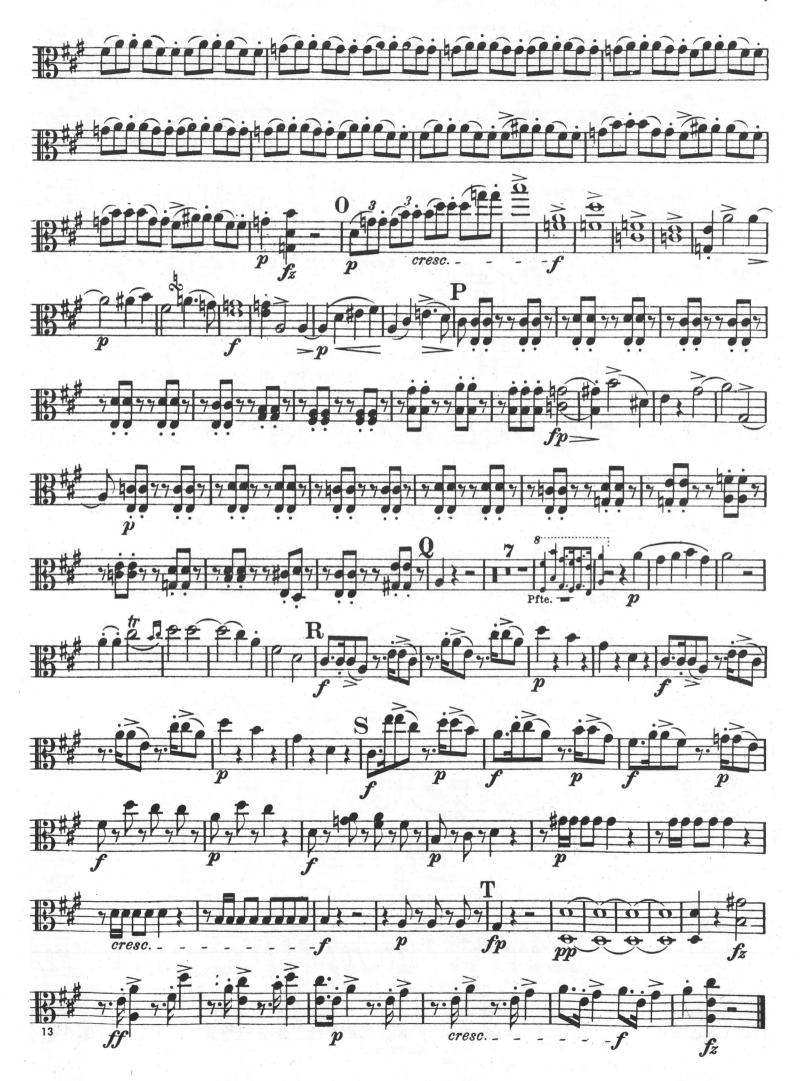

5

ANDANTE   4 TAPS (1-1/3 MEASURES) PRECEDE MUSIC.

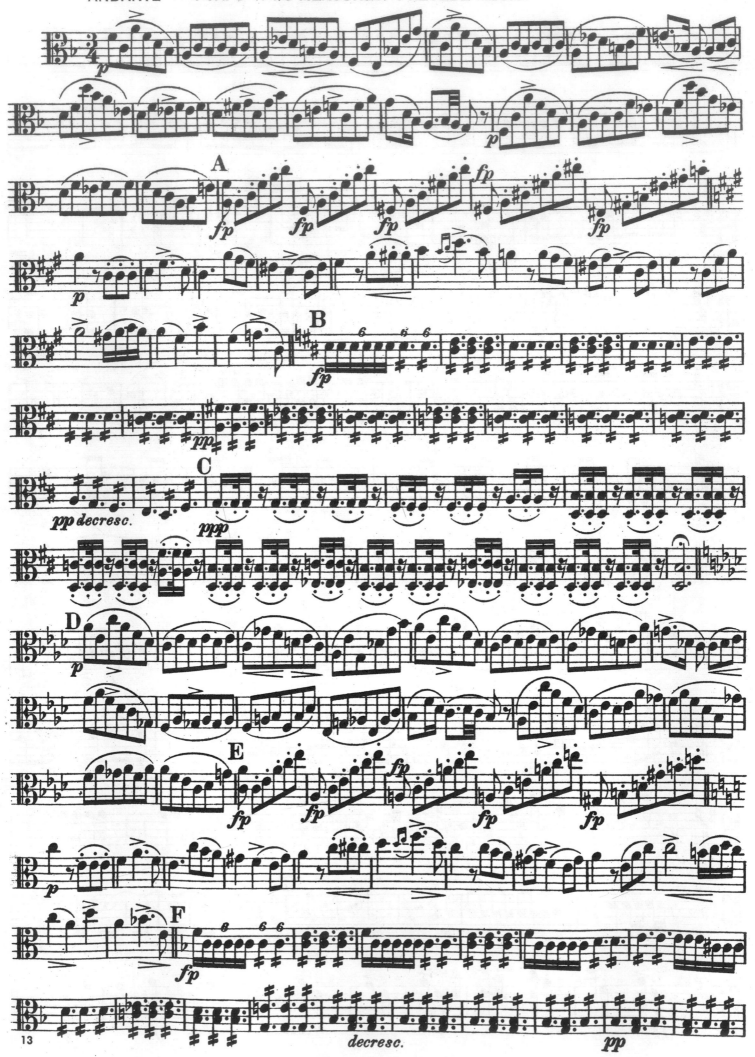

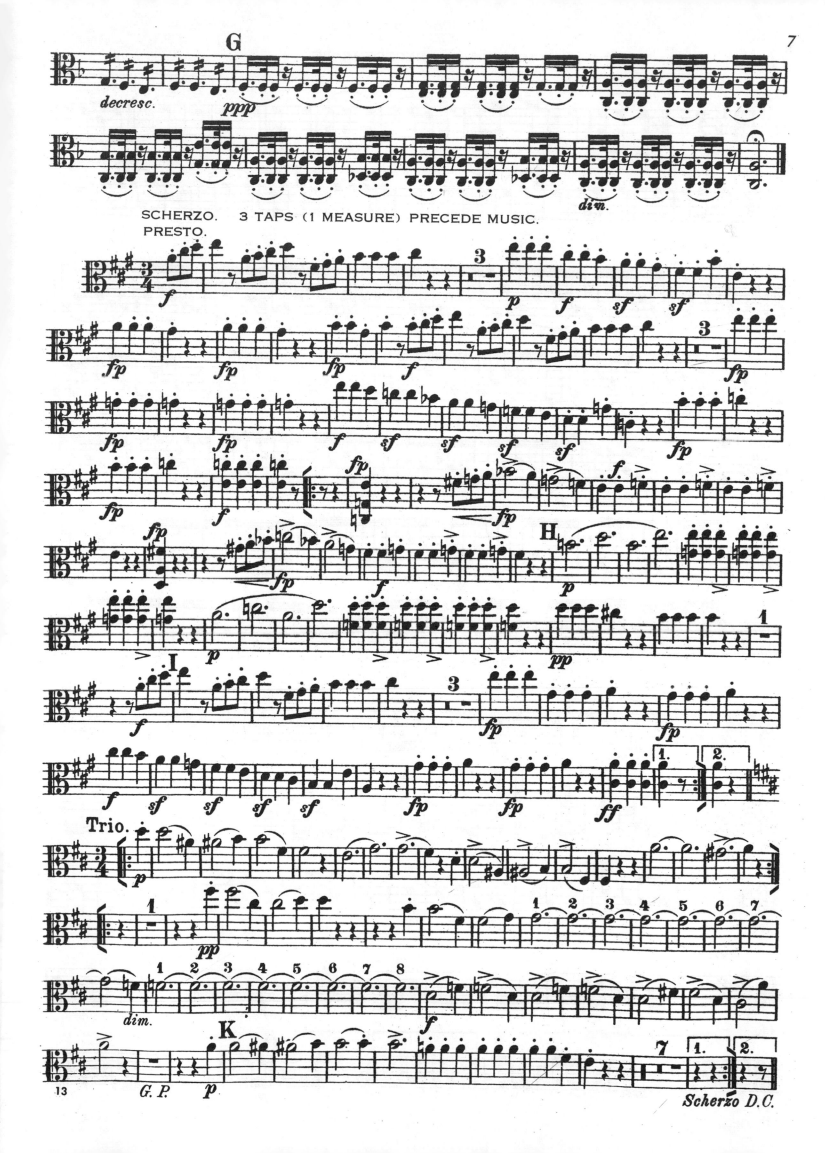

TEMA. 3 TAPS (1-1/2 MEASURES) PRECEDE MUSIC.

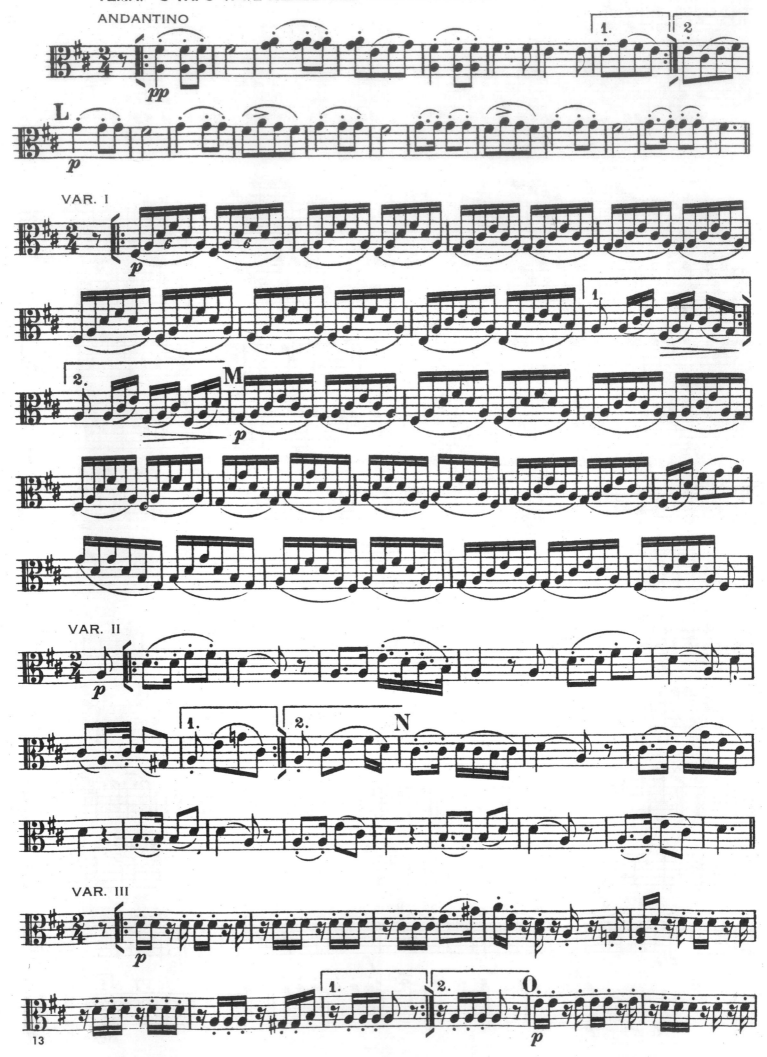

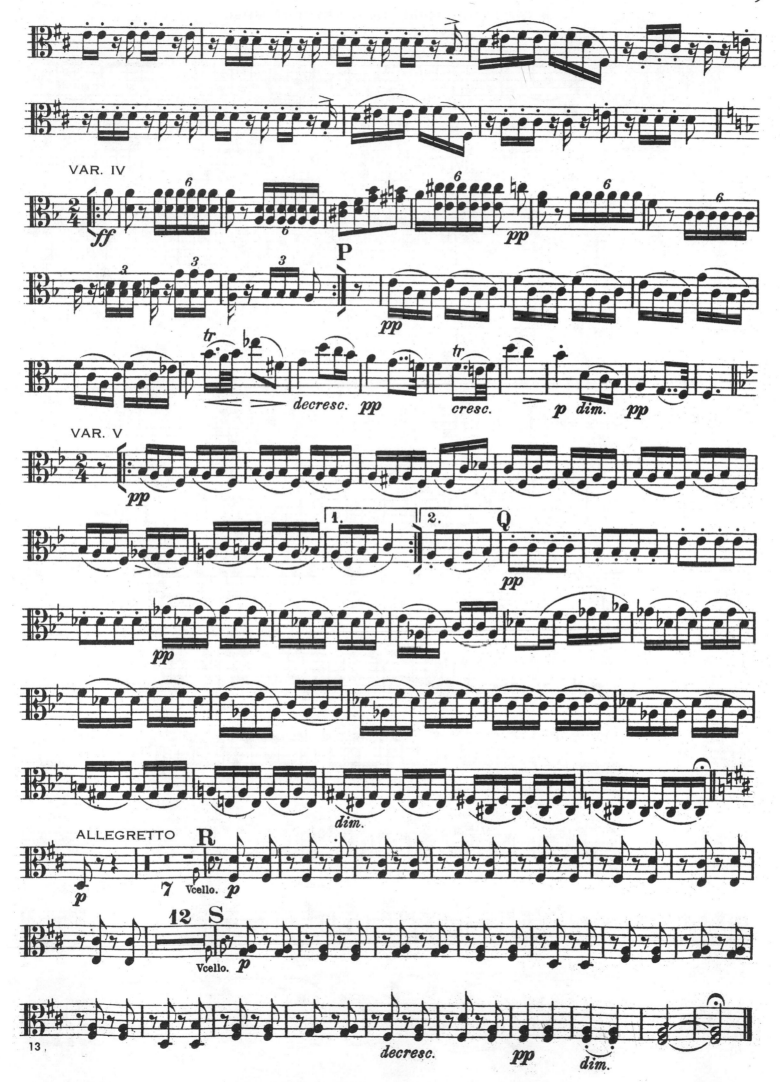

FINALE   3 TAPS (1-1/2 MEASURES) PRECEDE MUSIC.
ALLEGRO GIUSTO.

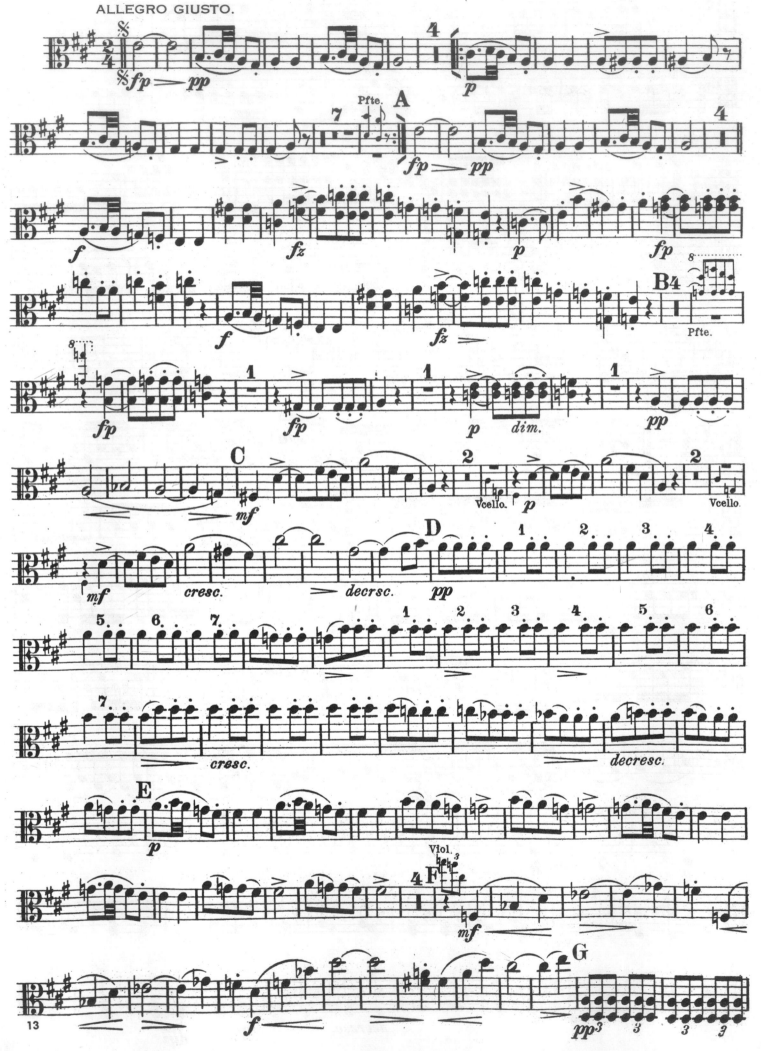

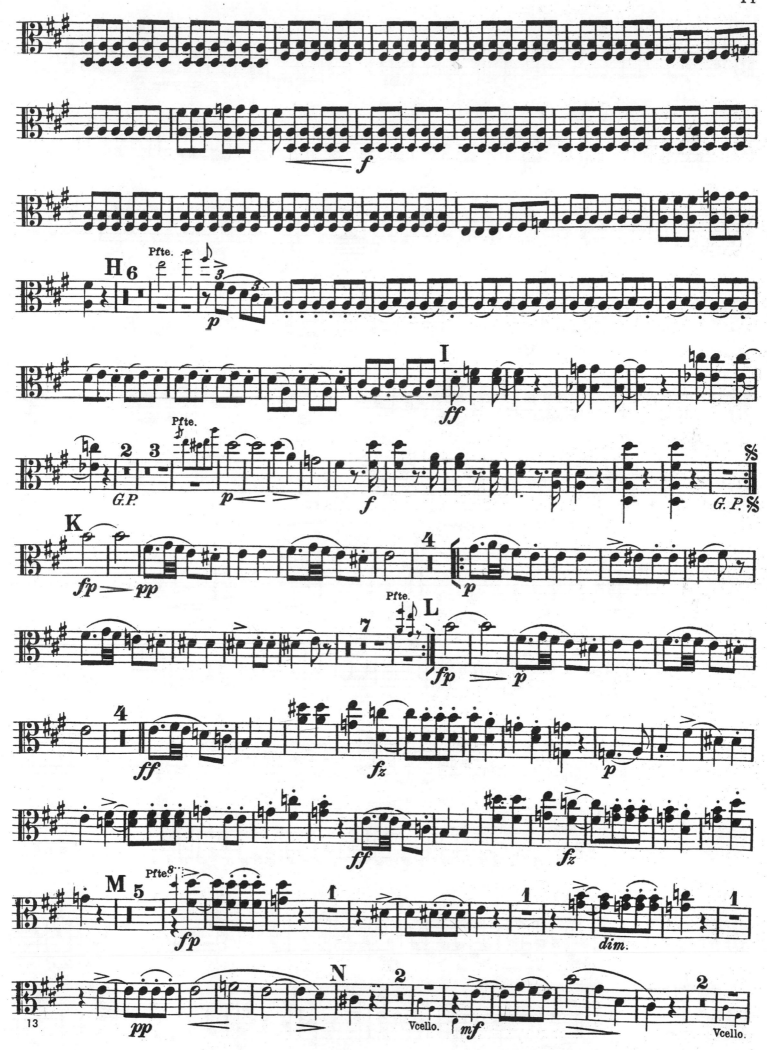

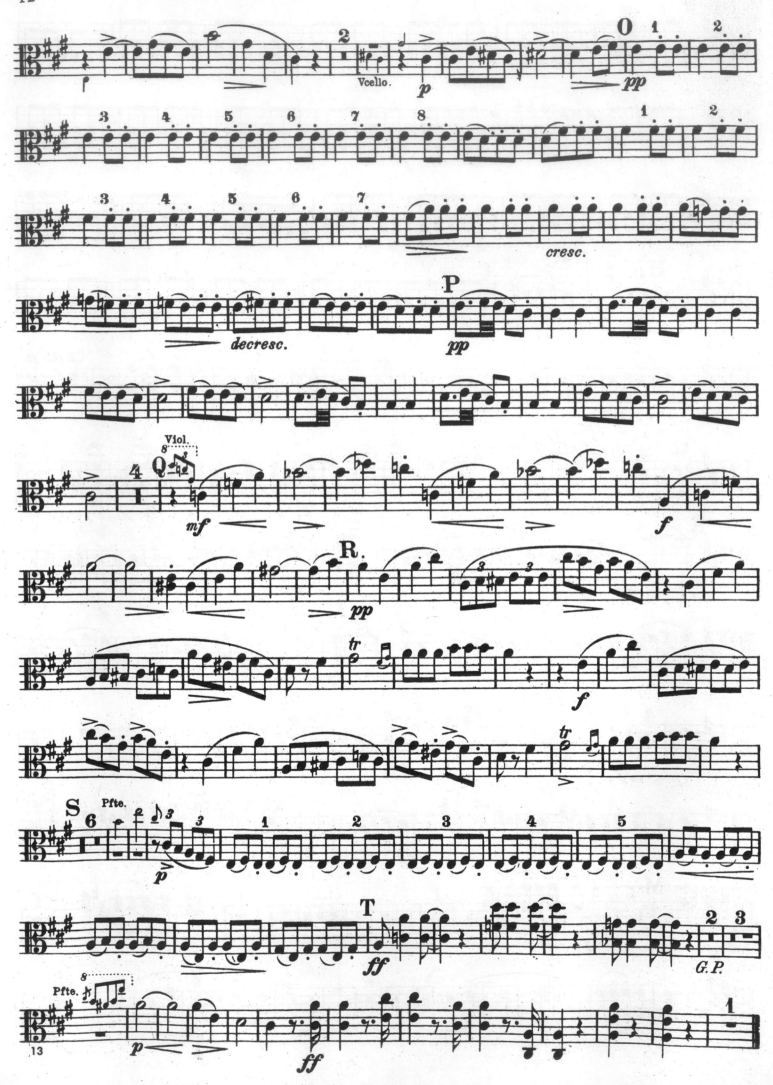

13